A Voice From the Hump

and

A Fourteenth-Century Poet's

Vision of Christ

A Voice From the Hump

and

A Fourteenth-Century Poet's Vision of Christ

John Wheatcroft

SOUTH BRUNSWICK AND NEW YORK:
A. S. BARNES AND COMPANY
LONDON: THOMAS YOSELOFF LTD.

A. S. Barnes and Co., Inc.
Cranbury, New Jersey 08512

Thomas Yoseloff Ltd.
Magdalen House
136-148 Tooley Street
London SE1 2TT, England

Library of Congress Cataloging in Publication Data

Wheatcroft, John, 1925-
  A voice from the hump and A fourteenth century
poet's vision of Christ.

  I. Wheatcroft, John, 1925-   A fourteenth century
poet's vision of Christ. 1976. II. Title A
voice from the hump.
PS3573.H4A6 1976   811'.5'4   75-38451
ISBN 0-498-01909-8

PRINTED IN THE UNITED STATES OF AMERICA

to
Mildred Martin

CONTENTS

ACKNOWLEDGMENTS

Some of these poems, a few of them under other titles, have appeared in AAUP BULLETIN, THE BELOIT POETRY JOURNAL, CAROLINA QUARTERLY, CIMARRON, THE DENVER QUARTERLY, DESCANT, DISCOURSE, EPOCH, THE FAR POINT, FORUM (Ball State University), FOUR QUARTERS, GARRET, ILLINOIS QUARTERLY, THE LITERARY REVIEW, THE MIDWEST QUARTERLY, THE NEW ORLEANS REVIEW, POET, QUARTET, SALMAGUNDI, SOUTH AND WEST, SOUTHERN HUMANITIES REVIEW, WEST COAST REVIEW, THE WESTERN HUMANITIES REVIEW, WISCONSIN REVIEW, WORMWOOD.

"Once by Seaside," © 1969, MADEMOISELLE, The Condé Nast Publications Inc.

"The Surfer," © 1967, The New York Times Company. Reprinted by permission.

Bucknell University generously provided the author with a number of opportunities to work on these poems. The MacDowell Colony and Yaddo hospitably provided quiet places.

A Voice From the Hump

and

A Fourteenth-Century Poet's

Vision of Christ

Part I
A Voice From the Hump

1
Retellings

THE RETURN

Home was a flop. The woman flatulent
and fat, wedded to a half-filled bed.

Before my eyes, the bitch, pig from a pup,
heaved to her feet, grunted once, rolled dead.

Well on his way back to boy, my father
imagined his arm could sling a spear.
It aroused a guffaw.

And my son, dear Goddess! a man
yet not a man, female infected, butt
of men's jibes, dreamer and dodger— phew!
unable to string a bow.

My beautiful people— palsied or gone
into shades. Their vulture sons,
pecking each other's eyes while I was gone—
a phalanx of beaks within the eagle's nest.

Over the palace, moss everywhere.
Weary my brain, fevered by songs
of swallows following from the south.

      Now sail is set, the tiller steady.
      This time my own skiffsman.

      Wind sputters, coughs, chokes on itself.
      Wonderful through this calm those voices close.

      Scars of the hawsers they'd braceleted my wrists
      and ankles with tell the whole story.

AGING AMONG THE SEVEN SISTERS: ORION SPEAKING

For Dennis Baumwoll

Those days... ha! in those days my brain
was a telephone directory with snapshots.

Exempli gratia: on sabbatical in '60
in a bistro in Trieste, despite the lines
and the dye, a girdled belly boasting (groaning over?)
two sets of children, I found the middle initial
that escaped her current husband (third), went on to call
the roll of "203" in '41 in alphabetical order,
within a couple of fingers of straight Scotch—
simple as naming the seven famous Sisters.

[18]

Secure, all these long gone sleep in their proper niches
in my mind, they resurrect in dreams. Sometimes
at night their *disjecta membra* reassemble
according to a novel order to recreate
one Polygnotus sophomore, my Merope:
Eve's ('45) serpent-reflecting eyes,
cheerful Leila's ('39) pouting breasts,
and the siren voice of Inta ('53).
In waking dreams they come back whole,
intégrited, true-named, not yet twenty-one.

These days— these days they're all one voice
between two lovely legs crowned with corn silk.
Them I've begun to look upon
as little sisters; lately even, daughters.
(Pfaaw! tchuu! incest, incest!
how to grow old— the harder to raise
the club— without corruption?)

Those days I forced myself inside
their pigeon heads, a rape they found so fond
they cockled me in their hearts. Before
leaving me full grown, a few I turtledoved.

Now, on this winter afternoon,
if, shrunk within my lion's skin,
I could call a name, if I should whisper, "Lisa..."

What's left to say? —except I told them true,
told the whole lore (it's all one story after all),
dared to its doing (first telling's always nearest)
as close as words can edge: the drunk boy's
ravishing; her father's vengeful blinding;
stumbling toward the better craftsman's clang;
a second sight; more loving and, her shaft

directed by the jealous brother god, a dying;
rebirth among the Seven Sisters here.
(Weigh loss the second, fifth, eleventh
telling; hundredth is told lie.)

A cold tongue charmeth not.
Aih aih, aih aih,
my dog did die.
Ah well, it's a job.

POET UNDER THE EAGLE

For Daniel Berrigan

> An eagle, having mistaken his bald
> head for a stone, dropped a tortoise
> upon it in order to break the shell.
> —Death of Aeschylus, *Medicean Ms.*

The herring gull whose three toes scored
this beach with anchors before I came
eyes me until I jump the jetty,
then scoots along the tide line—
stilt-legged, humpbacked *Deutsch Professor*
who likely dabbles in magic, flapping
with bony arms his motley cape.

Airborne, tucks his take-off gear,
which reappears as if by button when
he stukas shallow water caught between
the overreach of the wave and the undertow.

Scarce slacking speed, prehensile clamps
a clam, then boomerangs toward heaven.

My mind's presaging eye historicizes:
sunlight glinting off his alabaster head,
poet-in-exile sitting on a stone,
hearing the spondees in the Mediterranean surf
and watching bloodred water break to foam—
Agamemnon's gore become Orestes' light;
above, myopic eagle taloning a tortoise,
bomb-sighting on the shiningest rock below
for cracker; release and plummet, dull smack of shell
on skull; and all the soothsay victims of prey birds.

AFTER THE BROOCHES

For Harry Garvin

Points of those unhasped spears let blood flow back
the line I had been tracking. With her:
to return to the night that finished,
flesh bundle twined with veins, red rope
of her gore, I poised at the top of
dark's chute, heaved for a breath, my second life.

Round and slippy as I was I had to cut her keen:
still graver hurt to me,
expulsion from that garden through
her straight gate— a flaming pain.
Ooooooooh! cocky disenchanter of a city,
how I longed for my first wombing!

With him, still further back: passion to learn
my begetting, the primal act. Impertinent
his courtliness, rankling that reservation:
"A good king's scion, minion of a chaste queen
(you *are* whose child you claim?)
surely comes sacredly from Hera."

[21]

"No, no! Tell me, princely stranger,
man who must have fathered man,
before we go our ways, say: lies son
in the intent at that hot seeding?"
WAS I SUPPOSED IN LOVE?

Using the very goad he clawed my cheek with,
I riddled his skull; and left him bleeding.

Now pricked-out eyes perceive the two-pronged curse:
wanting and wanting to know.

IXION

Love turned me to it. Groin,
  groaning hub; head and arms
and legs, five flaring spokes.
  Self-rived, spread-eagled in
a swirling flame that lives
  off flesh without consuming.

My sex, the source— a nub
  of fire that feeds itself
and sparks those nerves radiant
  to my extremities,
wherefrom the blazing arc
  instantly is flung.

Hell beyond burning is
  the whipping of the brain,
the abrading of the pate
  and palms and soles, the veer
away from where I gist.
  I dream deep roots and anchors

[22]

and of all those stony women
   who support entablatures,
of heroes, gods, plain men,
   scarcely emergent from rock,
whose lives are frozen into
   plinths, pediments and friezes.

GAWAIN

Dying at Dover, blood from the old wound
got before Benwick of Lancelot
bathing the brassard and bare forearms,
still gauntleted hands of his uncle
the doomed king who held him, he remembered:

That moment on Orkney's scarped coast,
alone, facing morning, when he drank in
not sunlight nor heat but something more—
power strength force might main,
these merely names for what entered his blood,
made him seize a white rock his father-king Lot
and Agravain his full-man brother together
could not have budged and heft it toward that sun,
directly overhead now, feeding him like a mother,
then heave it seaward, out toward Dunnet Head,
where the whole vast southern kingdom lay.

He realized better than run home and tell;
but alarmed by his heart thump, his blood beat,
he stretched out and slept on the sand,
dreaming himself the favorite hawk
of the kingliest lord in those southlands.

When he awoke the sun was low fire.
Although he could tell by mere feeling, he tried
a smaller rock and could not. The tide
reared high. Inside the jaws of water,
wide before they closed, illumined by
a shaft of horizontal sunlight,
he saw three figures: a king mighty
beyond his father, who glanced askance
in sorrow; a gray-eyed queen who smiled;
a knight in bloodred armor, without
a helmet, who looked his anguished love.

The water mouth snapped closed. He turned
toward home. Behind him watching, a man
with a forked white beard and pits for eyes.

CAMPUS AFFAIR

Under a golden cape, her extravagant hair
flung over as she bends to him, his head
disappears; she's faceless too. One club-like tail
and six legs— two depilated pink, four

furry as the forest— depend from bodies
that concur beneath the tent she throws.
Little Red Riding Hood, all in yellow
today, crossing her German shepherd grandma

while diagonaling from the Literature Building toward
the Library, has lingered on the sward
to pet the beast and whisper in its ear:
"Those things books tell about you— I don't care."

Imagine that buttressed building is a castle,
that she, its lovely lady, has proved wicked
enough to wink the drawbridge portal
open and keep her tryst in a hard-by thicket

with a lycanthrope, while the baron
snores and fumes off last night's rouse.
Skeow! I nearly glee at the Dean, a Salem
judge's blood descendant, God knows

what mischief swinging in his briefcase—
behind that shrub you're passing, studied self-
possession clamped upon your face,
a blonde coed is making it with a wolf.

CHILDREN'S PLAY

The great grandfather of the bridegroom Prince
had been a deacon in my father's church.
They had the same huge nose. This coincidence
rendered his heroics comically absurd.

My daughter was the Purple Fairy— tall
for her years, graceful as liquid, a gossamer girl.
Thank Heaven, for the sake of Freud *et al.*,
she was a being from the *other* world.

The King once let the air out of my tires,
soaped our windows every Halloween:
quailing before his subjects' ironic "Sire..."'s,
his own court jester, derided by the Queen.

The Princess, frankly, was a disappointment.
Inclined toward weight and gauche, she seemed most passionate to
undo her fall of golden hair, smear oinment
on her pimples, don dungarees, and rendezvous

before the TV with potato chips.
But her wicked stepmother— a dark exotic thing:
sloe eyes of Sheba, Cleopatra's lips,
hair black and glossy as a raven's wing...

I was not forty-some— she was not thirteen;
all place this palace. Who would not kill a clown—
that sniggering King— to win this witching Queen?
like Antony, choose to lose a real world's crown?

YORKSHIRE FIR:
CATHERINE EARNSHAW SPEAKING

Red spurts no more from where he gashes me—
it oozes glassy. Great Chrütl! my skin has mottled,
my flesh goes grained and gnarled. I stretch my fingers— look!
before my knotty eyes they stiffen to needles,
point green, the color of hair mossed on my crotch.
Toes spread and twist, they clutch the under heath,
where my cloven foot has anchored. I'm on one leg;
my shade floats moored. Now all the consciousness
of what I was diffuses through my pith:
    I am that tree I yearned to swing upon;
      my voice, the moan of north wind through dry cones.

BEAUTY AND THE BEAST

I

No condescension shows, though she towers
above him as they talk while walking in.
Nor does he try to elevate himself:
his heels have not been lifted, hers are high.

He slides a chair— the height to be his perfect partner—
beneath her neat parenthesis.
Have they been sent here to torment me?

My guess is, fifty years this Atlas shrunk
has bent beneath the ball of flesh that willed
itself upon his back. From up here on a barstool,
the head of his that bears the look seems set
upon the table where he sits, severed,
on a platter, as it were. A beauty
maybe thirty, she'd tempt a royal beast.

II

What's wrong with you? you— YOU, not him!
You are the question mark, the crooked
exclamation. Don't tell me you're
a traveling secretary, guaranteed
a bedroom of your own! His sister, are you,
returning home to Daddy's funeral?
If you're for sale I hope you wangled yourself
a juicy bonus. Might he be a hypnotist?

Come on, come on, you can't expect to travel
publicly the way you are together and not
be thrown some questions. The world's not blind or kind.

Too much of man erect, is that the story?
you're piqued by difference? does oddity
amidst dull regularity excite you?
ennui's victim? do you expose hypocrisy?

Could it be you're cold and slow, straight-laced,
high-minded? and thus demand flesh flaw
to counter the elevation of the brain
and move you to the lower spheres of self.
His body— is it beautiful besides?
Do you idealize? your imagination,
does it straighten out? Or is his second head
a measure of the manly size and power
that you desire? Have you an upright
husband, another, normal lover?
Are you two souls the way he is two heads?

Beneath it all, YOU have to be disfigured.
Does hide and matted hair cover you knee to shoulder?
Do iguanas, snakes and fish tattoo your thighs
and belly? Have your breasts been surgeoned off,
so I've been lusting on an apparatus?
Do scars scrawl X and S around
your body? Has your torso burned and healed
a corrugated purple? Are you plastic-femme?
transvestite? changeling? Stowed in your luggage,
do you carry chains and whips, the Marquis' tools?

Tell me confidentially— does it yield
you extra pleasure? dare you touch it? fondle it?
name it and coo to it? curl your flesh around it?
womb it between your breasts and navel? does a voice
from in that hump cry, "Love me, love me!"
Is he your man because of, not despite?

Anticipation, does it bring a dread?
do you have to force a start, harder each time?
do you keep your eyelids clamped against it during?
is your peculiar triumph transformation,
breeding from grotesquerie the purest love?

Together do you crowd the heels of demons?
do angels weep for pity? what does the cosmos think?

III
Sick, sick, sick, oh, I am sick from speculation
on the practices of lust, the art of love—
a Humpty-Dumpty on a barstool, lady.

2
Sequences Open and Closed

WATER SPORT

FISH WISH

Hands handicap. Of what use
arms? Suspend, surrender, drift
the dark that's only current.

Why keep a head from a torso?
Impact the brain in the heart,
locate the eyes in the nipples.

Have all the lower parts conform to
a tail that's shaped to let the cleavage heal,
after underwater passing, without a trace.

The Fall was upright thinking; return
to prone. Why else each night
this wish to be a fish?

MERMAN

My skin is transparent as glass. Sargasso and kelp
tangle the underside. Lobster and crab

claw within my fingers. Seals slide my hands,
my feet. A salamander slithers through

my belly, wanting to be a python. Eels,
lightning-charged, wriggle in my brain. A groan

recalls my gulping of a tadpole, swollen
to bullfrog throbbing in my chest. My mother

hooked a lamprey between my legs; his head
is heart's form, he has a dimple for a mouth.

Killies and minnows dart the red canals,
they brood among the cells. Inside the liquid

sloshing the manshape membrane that I am
I feel the creatures coil, I sense them quick.

WATER GIRL

You lure me
          away from
                    dry land.

          inside you
Somewhere   a tide
        is heaving.

Who needs any eyes?

                the tips of
I swim in   my fingers;

from digits
          I dart to
                    a fish.

Emerging
          I gasp.

The rock you
              are sitting on
                          quivers,

          breaks into
its gray   the rainbow

(as through old glass the world ripples and colors),

your hair
          wets green,

one strand   like a scar.
          down your cheek

I try to
     come steady
              but shiver.

                    me back to
You are calling   the water.

[32]

OCEAN ONLY

and ever female is, for liquid being
is of infinite variety
under a sky— face facing face—
chromatically shifted and shifting by
hour and season; moon chaperons her,
frets her and lets her; storm cleaves her,
sun seeds her; time ago wind combed
lizards and Aphrodite out of her hair;
though most because in her you I
discover. And once enough I drowned
in you to find her there too.

YADDO BATHTUB

For Philip Roth

> Turn by an inward act upon the world.
> —John Wheelwright.

No Baptist parson's son who as an innocent,
though dissenting from the creed that dirt
is sin, got tanked religiously come Saturday night,
who at twelve was dunked in public to cleanse his soul
goes Diogening around the world when he's a man
for tubs of honest porcelain. Baths are my past.

At Yaddo, though, a bathroom is a *bath room*:
instead of a shower, a white whale eviscerated
and museumed, a gaping belly outsize enough
to swallow a Goliath Jonah, the Jordan dammed
and plumbed to purify the damnedest sinner.

What hardware! so lewd the gooseneck of a faucet
that Victorian gentlewomen for sure disrobed
behind a screen, then entered the water, drawn
to a depth to hide the shameful triangle,

in a blinding rush. Brass star-shaped handles
graven HOT and COLD might sluice the Gatun Locks.
For overflow a ditch of tile surrounds
the trough. That drain's the grinning mouth of Hell.

After so long, water this deep relieves me
of half my weight. I sound, I thrash, I surface
like a walrus; I porpoise-sport; a waggling seal,
I twirl the soap cake on my nose. For the ear
of the genteel housekeeper I bark: "I'm drunk,
I'm drunk in the drink, I'm drunk on only water!"

O Heavenly perspective, staring into liquid
stilled round my soaking body! As if this see-through skin
and profound dimension were the Looking Glass
of Alice horizontal. When my eye descends,
my flesh floats to the ceiling. If I acted out
my urge and walked on water, I'd have to giant-step
a lintel three feet high to leave this room.
The threshold's above the door; my toothbrush
hangs beneath its holder; a spineless towel
and washcloth rise erect; the shade pull perches
atop a string that seems enchanted by
a flute; uplifted from its antique fixture,
gas antlers electrified, a chain defies
Sir Isaac Newton. What wonder water held
within the john does not come pouring down!
Imagine bottoms-up upon the throne.

Stirring my little pinky, one wiggle of
a piggy toe— this place I haven't found
since expulsion out of Wonderland is gone;
it trembles on my will. Still-lying
brings it back. Amazing this power to save
a separate world by surrendering to the way

that water wants to be! I comprehend
how Nothingness declared the soul
of things to Einstein, fathom
John Keats on Negative Capability.

   Nixie, would you were here to lie and brood
   with me, after our fill of frolic
   and liquid love, at the other end
   of this water bed, our suspended flesh
   and breath fit perfectly to each other
   as twins in a womb. Why then we'd celebrate
   two sacraments in one: baptism into
   innocence reclaimed and water wedding.

CYCLE RETROGRADE

PLAINT OF THE UNBORN SOULS
All empty o o o!
   we're space cells,
      loops of light.

We own no dimension. Without
   belonging or belongings,
      save silence.
         Time ignores us.

Even liquid we envy though
   our craving is solidity.
      We don't know how
         to invest in stuff
            or how to do.

An act of love is what
   we're waiting for.

THE TRANSFORMATION

My head compacts with my body.
Whole blocs of my brain black out.
Nerves take command. I've
a mouth but no eyes.

Legs have rejoined. Who needs
any arms? With what grace I strike
and recoil! Unable to manage
a word, my slit tongue sizzles.
I shan't slough this snakeness.

FIRST FLESH EAT

The first time they ate the god,
                          pierced his flowering skin,
together sank dog teeth,
                     tore flesh from flesh, like birth,
ground him between hinged stones—
                              amazed, then shamed they red-
     dened;

through red they saw all red:
                        red streak the other's cheek,
red drool from reddened lips,
                     red spittle on the chin;

embittered by his taste—
                     not sweet scythed wheat,
a cheat, still it thrilled.
                   After messing, with heads
beneath their shoulders,
                separate they chucked in a thicket.

CANTICLE TO THE SUN

Sin was for profit to abandon that worship,
trade hot god for cold, living
for dead; betrayal of one gold
shape for nightly changes of silver.

*   *   *

This morning I'm keeping
the biggest sun I've ever seen
in my eye. Oh, to be Joshua!

After years of lunacy have I been struck
with Pauline vision? does freeze, ice, glaze
across the land magnify far fire?
Astronomy and common sense insist
nothing in the sky has shifted or increased.

*   *   *

Afternoon: west clouds breathed and blown
to the posture of a certain woman in blue
Picasso *fecit* loll above the ridge
recumbent as a Henry Moore stone stud.
Never will you convince me—
use meteorology, use geology—
something isn't up between those two.
With sun presiding.

*   *   *

Declining, sun's pierced by the spit of a cross,
it bursts, then bleeds the world. Wheeling,
I spy a steely moon on the rise, darkward.

Now that we've got it, snug in our pocket,
silver proves counterfeit. Life
is sun and the resurrection.

ICONOCLASM: A SHORT LONG HISTORY OF STONE AND STOCK RUIN

Five-tailed, graspable
more than tails because of
one's antagonism, they began it.

Chivvying stone with stone to tusk back at the boar,
hands found therein the god's head,
like a man's— head within head *is* stone;
aborting the point, they realized a nose,
one eye that never winked, no mouth— the god spoke not;
addressing the face, they smote with it no time.

Stone-skiving a stick to snug in the fist,
hands felt the goddess' breasts swell,
flanks flare, no cleave in her loins—
there might a man not put himself or want;
they abandoned handle for deity's worship.

Always in all those stones and stocks,
beyond pulse that quit and warmth
that froze, gods lived.

Then wrought in stone the miscreant hands a woman—
two each: eyes, nipples, thighs;
one each: mouth and navel (mortal proof)—
deapotheosizing hands, careless
of the old zones, defying whatever curse,
inflamed hands, sweating at mischief,
for deity homed hard in stone,
resisted invention, held eld's prerogative.

(The ancient truth before myth birth:
not one step back the steep way,
too curved for her straitened sense,
too hard for her soul-soft feet,
not ever started she up toward light,
never behind the fatuous plucker,
choosing silence to his off-tune,
loving him living the less, loyal
to the serpent who sluiced sweet poison in her.)

Rashly hands jimmied a chisel between joined thighs,
hammered home, cleft rock, through which gash
the god expired, yielded his stronghold.
That dint pierced the virgin boundary, violated
life's line, overflung the graven order.
Debased stone breathed and bled.

(The new lore taught:
Lazarus, who plainly he is dead stinketh,
from the rock come forth willingly.)

Soon, petrified by their handiwork,
they founded for stock gods a stone church
wherein they made of resurrection hard practice.

HERBAL

MARCH

Their prophecy bloomed, snowdrops
hang by the neck from green gibbets.

Yesterday, hairline cracks in earth;
today, swelling greentips
John-the-Baptist lilies' emergence.
Who has rolled back mud stones from these tombs?

[39]

To hear you acknowledge this month
as your birth time corresponds.

All week long silence misting south
above the river has been riddled by yawping,
the north sky opening on winging V's.

JULY

Sun this morning stuck
a sulfur tongue
through the mouth of a cloud.
All this green mocks me.

A summer afternoon comes back—
coincidentally your birth year—
when the fathomless blue Peace
on the other side of the world
tempted me from the lifeline . . .
suck of the latest kamikaze.

If only I dared give myself
to thistle, vetch and chicory,
could erect myself on trees!

Let me confess the worst:
my heartbeat quickened,
incitement deeper than grief,
when I knew my friend was a dead man.

NOVEMBER

Some time back the Lord God Black
sent Yellow, Red and Brown
infiltrating the Kingdom of Green.

Rags are pennoning omens
on skeletons of sticks;
like abandoned village women
leftover blossoms wait rape.

Last evening I crossed
the final butterfly,
a sneaker without a foot.

Remember that linden smell when
the end of the world was hyperbole?

Uncorrupted by use, a truant
boy hoards horse chestnuts.
How exemplary his greed!

DECEMBER

Around me here hump hills,
stalled herds of buffalo.

Wind lashes thongs of willows,
chafes bruises on white fields.

The morning of Christ's nativity,
frozen beside our garbage pail—a rock of a sparrow.

Five hobo dogs pad through the snow,
muzzle to muzzle. The old wolf pack.

Cliff faces sport Rip van Winkle beards,
while this quarter's moon, love,
is one pitted eye in some blind giant's face.

THEME AND VARIATION

LIGHTNING STORM

Supercharged, electrified, this atmosphere
(fraught with an aphrodisiac? infected with war
fever?) goes to the head of trees; can't bear,
these trees, can't without dancing— too much, too big breath for
them— dancing as though footloose, far wilder, flinging more arms
than Siva, oh! they almost lose their heads
doing this dance before storm. How it alarms, alarms
us! Lights needed to relieve day's midnight inside our sheds
blink astonished at their forebears: volcano wink-
ing devilishly in heaven's open navel, flaming spume
from sun quench (Cyclops' blinding), fire through a chink
in space. Hear surf, rampant to land, in sky drums' boom.
Under a tidal wave sucked high by moon, wait near kills
eye, ear, mind. Then water falls in hills.

CANTICLE TO THE TREES
I

Up there, somebody pretty big— Orion!
he dug a deep deep hole, in he stuffed
the sun, taking care to tuck all streamers,
completely and darkly covered he it up.

Sure and his hound pawed
the mound of space back in.

It gasps and blows, it
whistles, it blues and blacks;
and sparrows go-round-merry
on wind's wheel, doubleflap time—
the stroke of scullers sprinting home;
like tickled nuns they squeal.

Dance, you old earth dancers, dance quick
as the spirit breathes, dance fixed on a spot,
dance the dance of the many-armed, deep-rooted god!

II

In memory cleft time must engrain;
how slow no matter, such instant had to be,
that crisis in tree will,
will of this peculiar becoming,
when a mouth snouting underground,
venturing, straining for suck,
had to choose between time/space as home,
thirst impelling/integrity holding

>   squirm after water drop by drop,
>   worm transsoil every thirst?
>   thus dwarf all life down in footloose tendril
>   or
>   anchor fast despite,
>   wait always open to water's coming?
>   thus flower growth up in bole and leafage

ROOTED ECSTASY YOUR GLORY!

Besides, douses too the drench,
blusters too the blow
for His Eye's birds to wing it out in,
high and dry you provide.

III

Worship's way, dance implanting
men learned from trees.

[43]

BEDROCK ON HIGH MEADOW FARMS, FREEDOM, NEW HAMPSHIRE

For Patricia and Charles Watts

DIRECTIONS

Keep the late morning sun over your left shoulder
as you cross the lawn and high meadow,
your right foot always stepping on the heart
of the pigmy shadow you throw aslant the grass,
then crabgrass sewn with clover in second bloom,
prime goldenrod, joe-pye weed, yarrow,
and Michaelmas daisy, which flowers in August.

Climb through the wall, old as the Republic,
where the contingent strength of ice has rolled away
a stone the shape of a sleeping bear, invitingly.
Straight through a station of hemlock and cedar
you come on the water tank, a twelve-foot pole
with a net for scooping out field mice that float bloated
to the size of rats, leaning against it; beyond,
the dilapidated cabin where two in love
might live if one were a jack-leg carpenter,
the other could cook on an open-hearth fire.

After this dream, it woods you in— beech mostly,
some birch— so thick that when you check for sun
(over your left shoulder, remember) you see
light through a colander. On your right hand ahead,
the stunted shadow you are stubs on thick trunks,
shudders across roots, shatters on logs and rocks.
Sometimes the pieces submerge in green dark.
You're walking beneath a tidal wave, you expect to drown.

[44]

A clump of Indian pipe, which eschews the sun
and feeds on death, conjures young Emily Dickinson,
who found one shriveled bloom, classified among
the saprophytes, *Monotropa uniflora*,
pressed between the leaves of a pious tome
on God's handiwork, called "Natural History,"
taught by a Mary Lyon henchwoman,
before that afternoon in forbidden woods
bellying beneath Mt. Holyoke, she chanced
to touch the real wild thing with her naked sole.
Its white flesh tube so shocked her virgin senses
she ripped off all her clothes and wailing danced.

Verily, verily, the Devil's in that mushroom,
smoked black, poked up between the limbs of a beech
fallen in the pose of a dinosaur
who stopped and looked and listened
for locomotive time to pass him by.

The while you've been climbing steadily,
you realize all at once from the ridge
when the other side drops steep. Some halfway down—
a clearing you can't account for till you're on it:
a rock to make St. Peter gasp, Notre Dame buried,
the foundation, unquarried, of a hundred New England meeting houses,
huge earth bone bulging through soil flesh, a set
of granite thighs in whose cleft mass silver mosses.

Hedging the stone and buffering the woods
edged with scrub oak, a ring of creeping juniper,
which scratches. Once through the juniper, stretch out
on the moss bed. It's soft as the pillow of Venus.

[45]

LYING BETWEEN

Above, it's a day for the Second Coming—
no surprise to see Jesus step out
from among cloud flocks, walk down
this sky as liquid blue as Galilee, to proclaim:
"New Hampshire everlasting and unfallen!"

From there it's no far wonder,
just a pivot of the telescope,
to ants. Half red, half black,
each member of this nation—
as though that civil *guerre à mort*
Thoreau eyewitnessed and historicized
averted by miscegenation
that equitably proportioned
all its progeny. To watch
these wingless bees, pure primum mobiles,
scale moss Himalayas as a commonplace
reforms my sense of possibility with grace.

Bedded, comforted, I feel ease come,
I reconcile the while with my shadow.

RETURN

Who moved that sun and how?
I can't diagnose it now.

Though I know
my time is up.

So unable was my body
to impress the juniper?

All beeches grow the same,
all fall like dinosaurs.

[46]

The Devil never fails
to enter mushrooms.

And Indian pipe pops everywhere.
A ridge is a ridge is a ridge.

Let down by one leg, an ant
has five to haul his brokenness.

Had it tickled my chin and my armpits,
surely I'd remember such deep fern as this.

Now Heaven's obscure.
The way back's more.

ENVOI WITH APOLOGY
By the hour I cross the lawn, emergent
from the lower meadow, I've changed
places with my shadow.

There was bell-ringing enough,
tongues laughing at me tell,
to bring butterflies out of cocoons
before their term.
Now leaden tongues hang still.

"For returning late, disheveled,
and half beside myself for your party
in the garden, gracious lady, pray forgive me."
I had to get lost in Freedom.

3
Family Gathering

AUNT GRACE ALMOST

God willing, as my paternal grandmother who
almost became her sister-in-law would say,
my almost aunt, Aunt Grace, will start a new
century should she survive till New Year's Day.

She's an almost aunt because my Uncle "Doc"
(my father's uncle really, and her betrothed),
fresh out of med school, put his heart in hock
to her and Death, and could not pay them both.

After the doctor-lover squared his debt
with that Creditor who claimed priority,
for fifty years his almost bride from net
stitched veils for brides who really were to-be.

When I first called her "aunt" she was a cutie
of almost sixty, whose hair was maiden red;
a boy could see she'd almost been a beauty,
a man, she'd only almost gone to bed.

A Southern gentleman, with polished shoes,
handlebar moustaches, and a carbuncle
high on his forehead, kept after her to choose
to make him more than an almost almost uncle.

Though her almost meant his never, his passion always
waited. Did a voice from Heaven bid her shun
him when they passed along our upstairs hallways—
he fully suited, she bathrobed like a nun?

My almost aunt is almost deaf and blind;
for all who touched her life the losing side
of her rivalry with Death she has no mind.
My father, who when she was an almost bride

was the age I was to first remember her,
of three billion living souls is the only soul
she recognizes; even her Southerner
from a lukewarm memory has turned to cold.

For his almost aunt her nephew has one dread:
an unmeet termination. Which would gall most—
departing New Year's Eve and missing her hundred,
or making New Year's Day, belying almost?

VISITING HOUR

For Florence and Natalie Osborne

High above the city in a lounge,
nub-end of a spinal column— corridor and rooms—
I wait with Rilke's Book of Orpheus.

In 904 some vulture gnaws upon my mother-in-law,
brazenly, as if already flesh were carrion.
Life, desperate as when it raped
the single cell her start, wails passsionately
in her now, whose parenthetical span was dumb—
an irony she misses for the best.

Over her sheeted waste my wife sobs soundlessly
behind a smile as thin as gauze, her tears
as dry as pretense maimed by grief can wring.
Now daughter is the mother-comforter.

White-hooded Sisters of Felicia, gliding in
and out, render charity efficient,
though somewhat starchy, make mercy
incarnate, if capped with a little pride.

No breath of air stirs across the rooftops.
From canyon streets cut through these cliffs of brick
honeycombed for living,
children's cries, the wheeze of engines,
a closing siren, horns, clock's clung
float up the hanging heat.

Through a speaker I can't locate the Angelus
is chanted by a voice not man's nor woman's—
metallic benediction for this night.

I turn to Rilke— *Wolle die Wandlung*—
tense my ear to catch those rolling chords:
requiem for the lovely girl of twenty
who had just begun to dance;
death mass for the brown-eyed boy disfigured
by a squint though faultless as the Lamb—
dass du dich wandelst in Wind.

Does music lie like nectar
in the flower of all dying?

Through haze enveloping the city
sun suddenly exposes, poises above the entablature
of a distant building, while darkness crawls
over earth's edge, climbing out of ocean.
Then gored on pediment's point, sun
gashes, gushes crimson through the dusk.

The breeze that runs ahead of night
slithers my neck and cheek. "Let's go,"
my wife's voice whispers in my ear.

SEEING MY FATHER GET THE EVENING PAPER

To know he's in that box wherein he'll be
no more, swamped with flowers as he beheld
the crate that held what was his mother,
another what was my brother,
as he would want it strewed for us he left

to know he moves among those wiltless blooms
I know bloom nowhere
save where his fond belief
has seeded and nurtured them
against his transport into gardenership

[51]

would be to see him on the other side of water:
shining, free, returned, secure, at peace.

To watch him drowning in his overcoat,
leant against wind,
hefting each footstep off the viscid earth,
headlong into cold

an old man trying to run, refugee
from a shell-shocked century, blundering
his way through traffic as if
the buses, trucks and cars were bombs
dropped providentially around him

all unaware the eyes of now his only son
are looking out at him from inside one of them

the *Philadelphia Bulletin*,
in which he's daily read the world throughout
a lifetime without ever having found one word
about himself, rolled tight and tucked,
a monstrous thermometer, in his right armpit

drives me until I rage to rip
my sex off, hold it bleeding
in my hand like so much meat
for that dog Time to snatch
and tooth and eat.

LION IN THE LIONS' DEN:
ANOTHER FOR MY FATHER

The lion's mane's gone white,
  though scarcely thinner, and still
he paces: back and forth,
  across, around, whipped on
by his own raw nerves— a rage
  suppressed by bars his mind
has set in concrete. Eight times
  in thirty years this fury.

He gapes to roar— a wail
  comes out. Too deaf his ear
to take his own complaint.
  Every so often the tamer
who shares his cage, instead
  of her head, inserts two fingers
scissoring a pill between
  his jaws. Then makes him drink.

No more than Jesus, whom
  he fashioned in his best image,
knew he an earthly father.
  His Heavenly one was always
on his back, less blood to him
  but weightier than Anchises.
His mother left her father's,
  then her son's house no oftener

than Emily Dickinson.
  Unable to carry a tune
or bear a burden, she billed
  and cooed her life out to
the "lover of my soul."

My mother became her rival
in a deadly triangle with
    this same fleshless man.

His days stretch one dark night.
    Terrors pack his cell;
though substanceless, they all
    take shape, a single shape,
they all are lions— unmated,
    fatherless, stone gods lashed
across their backs, frenzied
    by the fear they'll eat themselves.

A TRUE RELATION

I

Ruptured from birth your heart was pushed to pump
so quick it tripped and flopped. I can pinpoint

the moment, backward from the telephone—
our father's voice, distant electricity:

"Billy [he'd never called you anything but
William] slipped out on us an hour ago."

—As if at last you'd done your one shrewd thing
in a life that otherwise was all one blunder.

You interrupted a martini. On the porch
up in the leaves where we collected to

confront your beingless, I scrutinized two flies—
never have I seen such huge flies— copulating

on the screen. Too much the father, too little
the brother, I would not let my sons watch tears.

II

My grief was not for what I'd lost— we were
no Castor and Pollux (not just because you had

another mother and nine years start on me);
were Esau and Jacob, rather. I grieved because

you owed yourself a life. Your only claim
to things extraordinary was your hair:

black gloss, all there at fifty-one. Whatever
you put your hand on withered. You were unAbel,

a vegetable loser. Unlike your brother
you never killed for God and country. I doubt

you committed adultery, though you had to marry
twice, siring five miscarried daughters.

Your TV's and refrigerators lingered like
Cain's incombustible turnips, while you gulped

pills, panting for bankrupt peace. The madness you
short-circuited into periodically,

instead of insulating you from currents,
shocked you to death. Even your dogs were nuts.

III

The night you died I woke my wife three times,
so brutally she cried and fought me off.

And in the morning flailed a tennis ball
with such blind fury I was easy prey.

[55]

RUMMAGE FOR MY BROTHER

"What is it, what's going on?"
"Today is the day of the dead."

"What *is* the day of the dead?"
"Something new they've come up with—
bringing them back on buses one day each year."

"All of them?" "No, no,
just those the living remember."

"How do you go about finding the one
you want to see?" "You simply have to look.
They haven't worked that out yet."

   Eyes unblinking, face after face as similar
   as fingerprints or fossils, their different-sized bodies
   strapped into seats, like babies in high chairs,
   not dressed for burial but in what looked to be
   their everyday clothes before.

   As we sidled up and down the aisle of bus after bus
   on that desert-like parking lot, we seekers
   kept our voices polite and low.

   I had my eye out for that dog-eared sweater
   he wore so fondly so long.

   A couple of times I thought I spotted it,
   but one turned out to be a child or a dwarf
   and the other, I think, a female Oriental.

   A metallic voice gave us ten minutes warning,
   as when a ship is about to depart. Somehow
   all of the buses got underway at once.

So far as I've heard no one found anybody.
Maybe by next year they'll have worked it out.

DEFAULT

I

Once able to swaddle you in my arms whenever,
doing so many a time,
I face you now across no crib bars.

Beneath the net that's stretched between us burns the pit
wherein those bones who wasted their own flesh
and gave themselves to fire,
from Abimelech and Ahitophel down to this very instant,
will never make the beginning of a fill.

Your self-styled sackcloth— dirty denim and frayed chambray
that mock the working uniform I fought a war in—
exposes me, immaculate in regulation whites:
the bastard son of Gabriel on Aimee Semple McPherson.

To meet your driven eyes behind the baseline,
to see your arm about to serve,
is to feel the cannonball you fire already.
Unmanned, retroactively unfathered,
I'll receive you.

As you drill my crosscourt back, your hair
flows Samson-like. Your vision tunnels so
on what you'd die to smash that you run blind.

The pillars of this Philistine community
are trembling in your grip; you and I are chained
for sport within a flimsy institution.
Your follow-through is natural.

[57]

II

Each memory you loft toward me
I have to put away; one missed
would smithereen me like a lobbed grenade:

    you in a homemade clown suit,
    a dunce cap *New York Times* you fingerstreaked yourself
    in orange, purple, green tilted on your head;
    beneath your chin, like a Fauntleroy bow tie,
    a 99 pinned by a deputy marshal (our dentist's wife)
    of the Halloween parade your kind march always prizeless in;

    you, Dave and Tom and Kit abreast
    down Third Street toward the monument,
    galoshed, ski(suited) troopers bearing
        two broomsticks (the younger Tom and Dave)
        one emasculated BB gun (Kit)
        one bladeless scabbard scored with
            some Masonic hocus-pocus (you)
    against an enemy still to be identified;

    naked behind our hedge one August evening,
    you and Dave, two sparrows, thrashing and squealing
    in a rain-warm puddle, a shred of Joseph's coat
    draped overhead— which muddy spree proved Paradise to you,
    you recollected once when you were old enough to know.

III

Unable to make my mind serve only arm and legs,
rather than scramble for lost causes in the deepest corners,
the closets, attics, nooks, and cellars of the successive houses
where you played and fought and slept, where hid and sought,
too spent to steady on my forebears' genes, my own,
so I might capitalize on faults and misses,
might learn from history and biology a proven grip,
some tactic that prevents repeated errors

(or purely for the knowing's sake,
for consolation, or to pass the time)

I flail away at my own heart with my own gut
(dipped, dyed in my own hot gore, and stretched)
in hope such home-aimed strokes will boomerang
from your side of the court to mine
some of the fury.

IV

Six games apiece in the deciding set.

"I'm sorry, Al, I can't go on. The sun's
too much for a man of forty-five."

CHRISTMAS GIFT

After presents, before our circle breaks,
to kill, assuage, indulge the pain
of come-back Christmas mornings when
my church-mouse father, providing barely
bread crumbs, clowned off humiliation
before mice kids at cheesetime,
I put a flute concerto (Christmas gift),
attributed to Pergolesi, on the stereo.

David, at fifteen flowing-haired and more
defiant of the Philistines and me
than Samson— I'm Laius, not Manoa—
highjacker of my liquor and bootlegger,
forcibily retired, for a clientele of teenyboppers,
bongos against the solo flute upon an ashtray
(an in-law's present destined for the next
St. Andrew's charity bazaar)
upside down upon his lap while sweating
out the minutes till we cut him loose.

Nursing a tyrant fury I watch the burning
of a rolled-up mile of Christmas wrappings
in the fireplace. Again we're at the crossroads,
son and father— my tongue a goad with barbs.
Before it can lash out, draw blood, I check
a "Cut it!" swallow so the points prick in my throat.

The self-inflicted hurt begets a wonder:
those tom-tom hands concerto in
the orchestra just as the virtuoso flute
trills out— a tempo so contagious
even the flames are twisting to its beat.
The contretemps of Lovin' Spoonful David
and rococo Battista Pergolesi
drives home how fierce I love this rebel boy.

4

Under the Circumstances

RING-GIVING:
A CEREMONY

For Gale and Manuel Duque

I
[He speaks]
All flowers bloom in rings
and every natural form partakes of
round. The loveliest of things
men make are truly love
spun out to curves and curls.
Our earth is sphere,
the sun and moon are
circle shapes of light. If there
are other worlds
far hence,

they must have center and circumference.
Unlike a plane, space
doubles back on its commence;
time too. Even
the way to heaven
abhors all narrows and all straights,
is ample, yet contains itself, like an embrace.

II
[She speaks]

An ancient legend tell us
                    when a lover wraps
her beloved's finger with
                    a band of gold, a vein
bleeds heartward from that joint,
                    from heart bleeds back again.
This lore tells more anatomy than body maps.

III
[He speaks]

Here in my hand I have a ring— there
lies within its compass nothing
now. Can you see it needs a finger?
Accept me as your lord, your giver of rings.

[She speaks]

With rings we pledge ourselves to loop
each other's heart; to join our family
like the petals of a flower; to choose
to weave our separate doings lovely
as all things that curve and curl;
to fit our being to a world
in space, of time; and at the end
to trust we've tracked the circuited way to heaven.

IV

[Both speak]

I unto you a ring now give.
From you a ring I freely take.
We plight ourselves for other's sake,
like gemel rings, as one to live.

By compact token
                   we stand revealed.
All we have spoken
                   is hereby sealed.

THEY SAY THE MUSE IS A WOMAN WHO HAUNTS YOUR CHAMBER

Only the cleaning lady visits my room
here— her hair a clump of seaweed
washed high upon her crown, able
to put forward a very few bad teeth.
Before you'd linger on her face,
you'd kiss a François Villon hag, in French.

Phew! she never was a beauty, though
there must have been that moment when
the butcher's boy thought her meat enough
to lay a hand or eye upon. Her fat tongue
slapped him down. Likely she sailed
through menopause at twenty-one.

When summoned by her knock, I plant
a foot behind the door. "Fresh towels
for me?" I blather through the crack,
"Change sheets today?" "Vacuum, mop and dust?"

"Mister," her cross eyes crow, "your time
runs backward while the world drives on, leaving
you in a study; it zooms toward Venus,
where the whores are softly blue, lovely
as waves and faithful as sequoias,
where the atmosphere is lighter than your booze.

"Mister, here soon you'll mince on ice
on icicle bones. Meanwhile, the flicker
against the beech taps a song more sweet than you
upon your writing machine, the clumsy coot
mocks wittier. Why wait? the jig is up!
You know what's left behind belongs to me."

LIONIZED

Forty-six and sick this year.
"Lovely lady, I'm plugged-in
to the sun." My father preaching sin,
armor against arrows of desire.

Too many words, too many words.
My sword is sleeping in my hand.
The spider's in my burning brain.
I try to love you, I try hard.

I know my father isn't well.
Nebuchadnezzar is my saint.
"Is there really any point
in stopping now?" *Of course I'll*

raise the money for him. Were there
ever green mountains in England?
Let's try again, again, again.
In the whirlwind but I hear

only the shriek of another am-
putation. What color is
the center of the earth? *I vis-
it him as often as I can.*

"My wife? what wife? I have no wife."
Space is a black hole with nothing
save time around it. Not coping.
"Who isn't in any shape to drive?"

I'm thinking of the children's fate.
A manicured and toothless lion
denned with some female Daniel, I'm
more than a little juiced tonight.

ONCE BY SEASIDE

For Joan

It began with that cable of seaweed
wind braceleted wet green around
your ankle. You beachwalked all careless
of the ornament— or were you coy—
until a tongue of tide unshackled you.

The herring gull we watched in quiet
terror was also involved: parachute
that never opened, dive bomber,
shiverer of sea glaze with
his ice pick nose, again and again
and again, always to catapult out of it.

[65]

Of course it came down to the night
and a bed blank as untouched snow—
yes, snow, in that apogee of heat.
And we became two bodies inside
one skin, thrashing like a cat
and a snake in a sack, declining
at last to a single pulse, a tide
without land for its measure.

Back outside our self, membraned
uniquely, how cut in half it felt.
When even lust lay dead.

While the moon out the window,
a stone honing blade edge
of night, struck star-sparks
all the way down to the water.

CHROMATIC SESTINA

The sugar maples bleed a hectic red
along these mountainsides. Some evergreens,
surfeited by sun's largess, are tinged with yellow.
Already oaks, which hold leaves longest, wear brown
leathery gloves against the hawk-claw white
that's coming. Frost has struck fall flowers black.

We must once more. Starting in pre-dawn black,
we head our headlights toward the flush of red
above the mountain. You can measure time by how white
the concrete comes; miles, too. Sunlight shows green
has given out. High noon highlights the brown
of this landlocked landscape; afternoon, the yellow.

Our stricken landlady rocks the porch, more yellow
than even a month ago, her brilliant black
eyes sunk still deeper in her skull. The brown
of cedar shingles, salted and bleached, tile red
of the mansard roof, brass hardware weathered green
are just as they were. Against the sheet's cool white

your breasts and hips expose a warmer white.
Contrasting yours, my unsunned loins look yellow.
In your waiting eyes I catch a certain green
that's not their color. Spread hair makes a web of black
around your smile. The sun bayside, a red
balloon, floats the dresser mirror, toning brown

the recesses of the room. Your eyes go brown
from where I've moved— sea window. I turn, see white
of splitting water windblow off the red
burst sun has blazed the ocean. Beach yellow,
hooking seaward north, declines into the black
horizon. Before I start for you a green

sickle moon snags my eye. Your eyes veer green
again up close. Within these minutes brown
has reached to where your hair now dances black
upon the sheet. I plead for breath as the white
wave overwhelms me. Your untanned parts shade yellow
in the darkness eyes come back to. No mirrored red.

From the porch stairs stars spark green above the white
foam and brown beach. No surprise in the yellow
face as we leave in blackness. Now moon's blade's red.

DRY STORM

A stilted playhouse dark
beside the ocean.
Now and again an unseen hand

would part night's curtain.
Light gash disclosed nothing;
the final act would not begin.

Backstage thunder echoed hollow—
a sucked-out eggshell of a storm.
How could there be belief?

Waiting out the time
by the glass wall, I
had no more will than sand.

From where you lay awake
you must have heard
the yielding of the door.

A word impossible to give
would have drowned that puny surf sound.
In my going there was no daring.

TO J., WHOSE PARENTS FLED THIS EARTH
WHEN SHE WAS VERY YOUNG

Until you let it leak through bourbon neat
    I never knew why
at certain touching times you seemed
    to tune in voices
that to me were riddles in a bond of silence.

Some might argue it a rotten trick—
        transporting you here,
all that distance from soft dark to light,
        inside hot to cold,
then cutting out to let you cope alone.

You comprehend it better than to blame:
        chaos in the cells;
one lapsing step beyond a lifeline;
        bomb in a bedroom;
some engine run amok, a star, or mind.

Now I understand you sometimes focus
        on the holes in eyes
and crave a warmth past flesh, chilled
        by their afterbreath.
How fierce my want to unorphan you with love.

SUNDAY MUSIC

Taking the air in snow that was unpredicted,
        which transforms shrubs to ghosts,
listening to calls from leftover birds my ear
        fails to connect my eye with,

gasping at the proclivity of the alder,
        whose precarious hold on earth
is driven home to me by the slant of flakes
        and the way a shove of wind

deracinated a straight sound spruce last week,
        I feel the cords between
me and the world stretch to near breaking, I go
        unmanned this Sunday morning.

[69]

Sunday! Bells amplified from far remind me
    I'm an excommunicant
believer, bereft of my father's consolation
    though unrelieved of guilt.

By the time the morning service would be ending,
    snow has turned to rain.
A voice less living than an echo rasps
    "I lovuh you, ba-by" from

the transistor Rachel clings to for a friend.
    My blood begins to sob
at the progress of God's images from
    flesh in a Garden to

nerves in a plastic suit. The mannequins
    showing the fashions of
the *Times*— empty beauty of human forms
    recreated out of

torsos, heads and limbs scattered in fields
    and villages by bombs
machines, brained by willed instruments, have seeded—
    mock our Lord's Day conscience.

Not until midevening, halfway through the fifth
    of six Quintets by Mozart,
does your Real Presence, Love, embodied in music,
    allow me to own my flesh.

GRIPPE

A squint toward the slit in the drape
informs you that sun is performing
heroics outside after last night's ice.
Under blankets you don't care.

Blood's roused, it blushes;
flushing, it blooms to a rose
in whose petals you lie like a beetle.
This heat is palpable, a glove or a lover
that warps on your body. A tabernacle
within a tent, it caresses, comforts.
In this Holy of Holies something glows,
a Real Presence. You submit to the dark.

Such swaddling recalls another being
in another time. To return, your body must go it
alone. Estranged but loath to bed elsewhere,
mind occupies the adjacent pillow,
tentative as a dimple, will-less as an egg.

Thrusting an arm or a leg to a cold spot
on the sheet is rape. When your pulsing can
provide all the movement you wish for,
why bother a finger or toe?

From some place across vast water float
voices you almost recognize. A name
stirs a nerve that would circuit a picture
if your ear attached to a brain.

Rattles, rustles, thuds rise and drift
like smoke off something being handled.

[71]

Solaced by its envelope, your body
makes up with your mind: Come back from that pillow,
old pal, and join me in the grippe.

You're a fish in a hot hand, a tongue
in a mouth, being but unborn.

5
Each for its own Sake

THE SURFER

rides a rolling pampa astride
an untamed stallion who
bellies too deep for a girth;

kneeling in rhythm he plants
one foot, more gingerly the other
on the high-heaving back;

drawing on reins of mere air
he uprights, then inches on toes
and the balls of his feet toward the mane,
as if ocean were trained for the circus;

    flung foam scuds wind,
    the beast rears and bucks,
    green swallows hove rider.

[73]

IN HALF LIGHT

I

Some lights move perceptibly. Though the sun
is down without a moon, half light tonight
dies slow. Above, a weight of snow for tomorrow.

The folk afield are always turning to bone—
a matter of time. No lines made by minds
or fingers can catch the ebb and the flow.

Where, oh where in the world a word as alive
as wind through wheat just before cutting,
when every grain hair rustles— love's prelude,
the very sound of undressing?

II

As if this must or that
adds up to choice, as if
you will the needing or the not.
Ditto the wanting.

You sigh: it is my life,
my very life, my only life.
And others, others?

How ever balance the deadweight of pain
on the opposite end of the seesaw?
the final jolt to the falling? the hurt
in the one left out?

(Pftuu! a woman's soul is my Achilles' heel.)

Yours then to lie tonight
with love as a skeleton
beneath the sheet.

[74]

III

Shall I, will I
give it or give it up?
let it or let it be?
shall I give? shall I let?
ought I let it then be given up?

More frail than water-stretched webs on grass
of a goose summer evening, the lines that weave
the life-work. Confession's a threadless needle.

And the heart complains, I can't, can't feel,
can't feel anything any more, not feeling
is all. Poseur, fraud, bawd! furies the head.

IV

O for those who drew it out in blood with a spear
of their own making, graved it into stone, danced it
on a hilltop against the sky! Some of their motions carried,
we know, down wind into images that live.

V

How can the scratchings of a peacock in dirt
and dung, the underside of preening, no matter
how fortuitous, justify you?

What can words ground between teeth
working like mills of sin, reclaim?

PARENTHETICALLY

I

o: for a wreath of singed hair,
the lips of a gun,
cats nose to tail circling
a treed man, the fourth vowel
doing itself to a mouth.

II

Seeing a young wife with
a clothespin between her teeth,
draping a sheet, I recollect you.

How in morning frenzy your eyes
decline the names of all the colors.

III

Wind tumbles pear blossoms,
plays familiar with fern.
Orion sucks his thumb

while yellow boys die on TV
during dessert and coffee.

IV

Circumstance closes, insidious.
I crave, crave something ceremonious.

V

Even these words to you,
quieter than spoken, are faults.

Bitterly my tongue has learned
how sweet the flap of silence,
envelope of a poem.

THE DOMESTICATION OF TRAGEDY:
OR
IN DEFENSE OF MELODRAMA

The languor of the tall grass on the dune
measures the scant of breeze this hour. Noon sun

doubles its light upon the polished flat
of ocean. Theatrical! A brindled cat,

silk as a tiger, pokes whiskers against
green stalks, one at a time. His left eye glints

like our closest star. A monarch butterfly,
more striped and black and orange hung in sky

than the covert cat, nibbles some fumy sweet
pocketed in air. Wings scarcely beat.

Between two blades cat whiskers stop and tense:
no jungle drama conjures more suspense.

EACH EPOCH HAS ITS FIGURE

I

No longer the journey; everybody
travels these days— vacations to the moon.
Cheap and nasty, a house dilapidates.

See all their lips move
on the other side of the window,
shaping words you only read:
let me give me take me.

Faster than decay desire
buckles, wilts, one day lies flat,
a shadow you trample. It cares
no more than bricks can know.

We are nobody else no other where,
we are here in this falling house ourselves.

II

I'm so dry behind the ears
I flake. Paint peels,
plaster cracks, floors sag,
the foundation sinks. Pftuu, those little heaps
of sawdust, gold piles beneath the studs.
If Flood should come . . .

III

From this time on
whenever you answer the door
or go out among people,
be sure to carry an ax. Let them
stare. Even violins have turned violent.

And one of these days when
you find yourself a turtle
without a shell, you'll know
to go where fir trees grow
needle to needle.
That will be your first journey.

Discarding the ax,
then shoulder a spade
(never trust a gun)
for when you reach a clearing.

It will prove too late
to make a story of.
Meanwhile you're stuck with the house.

THE HUMAN BUSINESS OF METAPHOR

> Art pushes anybody who is possessed by
> it to relinquish his own personality.
> —Gustave Mahler

I

You heard the doctor say:
"See yourself as you are,
naked before a mirror."

Not in a cube of mirrors, making love,
nor before an oval looking glass on a stick;
not with pictures of yourself studding the walls.

Study yourself naked only to see through,
so that no longer will you know
your own face,
your very body,
even by their scars.
He meant, see to forget yourself,
unknow, as though you never were.

II

The mirror has yellowed, darkened,
scored in particular corners of my face.

Each year when the sun runs into
the open jaws of the Lion
there's less to deny.

WHY THE FLAGPOLE SITTER

If now, while fixing his eye on the icon, he walk from west to east,
he will find that its gaze continuously goeth along with him, and if
he return from east to west, in like manner it will not leave him.
—Nicholas of Cusa

It's alive but the cat
                         in the window does not dream
nor remember, looks
                     not at but past.
The more do trees
                   and flowers and moss.

In those days we stared
                         agape at the man
atop the flagpole
                   between the lake
and the ferris wheel,
                       alight all night.

Why such integrity from one
                             shafted by his boosters
as a stunt? Suppose that pole,
                               earth's axis, protruded
equally in China,
                   supporting his brother;

suppose our hemispheres
                         are only Siamese twins,
that pole their manhood bonded,
                                 erect, on top of which
some self they've found or made
                                 sits posted like the cat,

watching unmindfully,

                    waiting without wanting.

How else account for

                why the flagpole sitter

wondered us to

          wonder in those days?

VASE AND IVY AS OBJECT AND SHADOW

I

A wall of almost white behind a vase
of true white porcelain, containing ivy:

the shadow of the vase that holds the ivy
projects upon the wall of almost white.

II

Wreathing the vase are leaves of several greens,
upon the wall leaves take a single tone—

near black, above a table purely black
whereon the vase of ivy stands behind

and to the left, slightly, of a red
candle in a pewter stick: not red

but orange-red and blue the flame
(the red of the candle makes this clear,

except that at the top where jet
illumines, wax is orange-white).

[81]

Still in the vase, the ivy as
projection shivers upon the wall

as if a breath transpired from the leaves;
the stirring spirit is the life of fire.

IV

Upon the wall of almost white the leaves
loom larger, stems broader than in the vase;

there ivy owns one plane, leaves
overlie, the shadowed vase shows flat.

Out of the sculpted vase, some leaves lean toward
me, some away; stems curl dimensionally.

THE EYE AS MIDWIFE

Your sleeping flesh, naked
                    on a couch (green of fern),
curls intimately around
                    the gist of your being— sequence
of curves, concentric, diminishing:
                         hip calf shoulder breast cheek.

A pink tube of light,
                    transpiring the lens
of the bull's-eye window,
                         mouths upon your belly—
all the way from the sun
                    mothering out warmly this morning.

Where find the father
                    necessary, sufficient
to surgeon a rib,
                    then flesh it, inspire?
I'm agape at your waking,
                    my left eye Rubens, my right Renoir.

FRENCH POSTCARD:
NU DE DOS

Naked before what looks to be a tombstone
on some azure planet, her flesh is one
with its ambience: the mottled blue of
old postage stamps wherein an eye
can detect as in marble, maps of anything
at all— except that one thigh, viewed
from inside, is deep rose.

The suggestion of her posture— a few strokes
did it— you knew would pique and arouse me:
bent back begging a palm or a whip;
face hid, from grief or shame, in a basin
of arms; feet fakir-tucked beneath
her lovely butt, as a pillow or fleshy dildo;
right knee, into her mouth, spread from
its twin at an angle that forces one's eyes
to ride to where thighs home.

What your hand posted me from France is ink,
unsubtly blued and impressed by a fist
of steel upon glossy paper— realities
removed from lines and tones, washes
and swabs Picasso's seeing fingers teased

out of the model and onto tentered canvas.
Please know, a moment ago when she caught my eye
askant, unmindfully, my fingertips
made flesh of only air.

ENTERING MADAME BOVARY

I

Hm . . . hm . . . [throat clearing]
to begin:
   My love and I trod . . .

What a howl! You never
trod anything.

   My love and I . . .

Come off it— you never
had a love.

   I . . .
No, you never.

     entered Emma Bovary once.

   Nests in her armpits
   a mane down her belly
   shag on her gams
   and a pencil-line moustache

   she worked so hard
   sweat pearled on every hair

into her ear, rather well
chewed, I whispered
pretty things in Provençal,
prepared for the occasion

her breathing when she came
made me fear she'd swallowed glue

her eyes lit up with jacks
of hearts and across her chest,
flat as bad prose,
RODOLPHE WAS HERE glowed crimson.

II

Starting out of my latest dream
I smothered my face in the pillow, went blind,
smelled and tasted cloth and feathers.

Had Emma seen me then
she would have giggled.
"There lies a man with a pillow
for a head," she would have said.

So many years ago
you can't tell read from real;
and has taken more than some
are granted for shame to act.

III

Did entering Madame Bovary
teach you anything about the dying arts?

Afraid not. The better the lay
the less one seems to learn that way.
And Emma was a something,
despite some initial audio, visual and tactile
disappointments. Of course, she lived before *science appliqué* made
　　　　mannequins;
you know old perfumes fail in crisis.

Well well well, best lure
some inept whore in your door.
Else grow greedier with age and rage.
At a certain time of life
you really must start learning how not
to live, must practice it like prayer.

All this is written in a letter,
self-addressed, instructions
for when to open on the envelope,
which you'll find right where you placed it
years ago between two certain leaves
in the calendar of your life.

Ah, yes. That message from the past.
I'd forgotten. Emma gave
too good love, after all.

6
Some by the River

AFTER THE *FIN DE SIÈCLE*: CONRAD ON THE PLANK

Hueffer presents himself as a good soldier,
a landsman who never nods. I note this with no
rancor. Too wary an eye to be seen
without first seeing, blood too proud—
Teutonic, I almost said— to be caught napping,
too excessive a man to own need.
Each day I'm farther at sea.

Sometimes one can feel the words
trying to enter the cells, like poison
or germs. I envy the urchin—
his purposelessness, disability,
lack of inclination or use; halfway
to stone he is living shell, though barely.

[87]

Rats have run of the hulls.
My my my— how many wrapped in sail!
While the oldest man in the world can never die.

Sleep cheats, I concede that, dreams thieve;
still, awake is a fake. And the cost, the cost!
So, one nets a life, threads interstices.
To dive deeper than words, or images.

My lines go slack. I'd buckle,
curl like a wave round the globe,
I'd make a wake through space,
shrink to just center, slough
circumference, I'd become a Pole.

Two states grudge each other,
rival, bristle, arm, invade.
Sand is the no-man's-land they fight
over in. The battle seesaws, *guerre à mort*.
Sometimes men, certified flesh, expose themselves
as stowaways in cabins on some remote ocean;
beyond the pale they are trying to force the assent
of the self, which declines, remorselessly.
More often some shape from the deep will rout
a piano or thigh, reduce a chart or chronometer
to chaos. The plank has begun to tip seawise.

Not reality perhaps— for how can one tell?—
but the sense of it at least,
which may after all be all, comes and goes
like tides. More like light or fog
over water, the pressure of air suspending
red mercury. Except that one's soul
originates this weather, generates phases.

As for my horror of mirrors: you must believe
it is not that the beard makes me *à la mode*
nor that I boggle at this shape or that
of the Protean monster I cannot deny—
rather, I have finished with reflections.

ST. JOHN SPRIGG, PSEUD. CHRISTOPHER CAUDWELL, 1907-37

For Karl Patten

At seventeen he exorcised God's Graciousness,
unmanifest to him who manifestoed
doily culture's dying into physics.

Kissed home good-bye; and read himself.
Dried blood, which held all history's books
together, would not write his poems.

Misty those days he stood evangelizing
in the Crisp Street Market, apostling at the Tube's mouth—
real monument on illusive ground. The tracts
he hawked were hacked from St. Marx' gospel.

Promiscuous paramour, so rudely jilted by
the loveless he solicited— men shat
out freighters' bowels and vomited from underground—
he turned his back on Poplar, drove through France
in an ambulance with a gun to Jarama,
where some he loved he had to kill because
they would not love. When Caudwell died
a martyr, St. John was born again.

ONE-WAY CONVERSATION WITH RANDALL JARRELL

I

You are not expecting, I know, pale horse,
pale rider to come clopping along the concrete,
damming traffic and rousing horns,
or ambling diffidently on the shoulder,
lingering perhaps to forage clumps of grass
the highway crew has missed, for champing.
(Imagine, an *Erlkönig* on the berm!)
That was in once upon a time.

With it all you sit smiling: black fedora
cocked rakishly, bearded like a Nubian billy goat
(though you are Taurus), your wristwatch giving
away time, among milkweed, wild carrot, thistle
on the hillside of this boneyard above the freeway:
SPEED LIMIT 60
TRUCKS 55

II

His style precludes a snorting diesel;
a hearse would broaden irony to farce;
an ambulance reduce it to mere prank—
besides, perhaps . . . nor either a preacher's car
or a chauffeur-driven Cadillac— God, not
the black of false humility
or of crudely understated power.
No, no, your eye is *qui vive*
for a whore's-cheek red convertible,
roof furled. Perversity will provide
a delicious day on earth.

One sign will be the Rorschach on
his parchment forehead: a chance splash
from the missing-its-aim inkhorn
of the *Ehrwürdigen Vater Herrn* Martin Luther;
you'll read the mark of the Beast.
Another will be the blonde lolling
beside him in after-coitus sleep,
a smile on her lips for the poet who
imagines he has had her. Of course
her forsythia hair will windblow.

From the time you butted on this spot
he has been circling, bidingly:
A Dog in a tub on wheels who was the Morning Star.

And when, as it must, your eye recognizes,
when your will, as it will, staggers
among the options, when your nerves trigger
from final disgust at being in form,
he will, sensing it, whisper (so as not
to awaken his lady): "Now no more terms."
Hearing above the Hell-hound howl
of the motors, you will answer:
"Signed and sealed for good neither
in blood nor ink but in my life."

III

From that bank the drop is fast as any cast
from temple's pinnacle, as plummet
from womb of plexiglass five miles aloft.
Your timing will be perfect:
before you can smack on the concrete
you will kiss off the grinning engine (you hate)
into the world (you love) of black swans.

FLOWER PYRE:
WHEN ROETHKE DIED

On the backside of this cemetery,
unplotted land beyond gravestones,
concealed behind a wall of spruce
and hemlock, smolders a heap
of worn-out greens and blossoms.

The fetor, stinging stink, smacks
me across the eyes, makes water.

As if the flower flesh inside old Otto's
greenhouse— earth's clerestory, vast
cocoon of glass where green worms
butterfly— fumed like a city dump;

or that citadel in the sky,
all those centuries of cantilevering
by our ablest architects of the abstract,
exhausted to smoke.

Wire backbones of wreaths and sprays,
black snakes in white ashes, survive.

DE BERRYMAN'S POSTHUMOUS *DELUSIONS*

Enraged for love at Jesus and Walt Whitman
he scraped left cheek, that side his chin
and wattles clean as a turkey ready
for the pot. Then corked shaved half his face.

That grand old clown John Berryman
stepped in a pee-and-sweat-stained union suit.
From the trunk he stowed his dearest gear in

[92]

he plucked a parasol (for style and not
for dryness when he'd walk beneath the water)
and tiptoed toward the wire he knew was not
across our great divide far north of Huck and Jim.

The silk-on-bamboo-wimpled single wing
that could nor fly nor float
he opened with a fillip.

Such quick descent so fast, because his head
hung heavy on his heart, the thing wrong-sided
out at once, up-cupped into a crocus,
its tassels exclamation points of horror.

Betting no net to save,
no swooping arms to bear him lest,
he cried "Mary Mother Mary" all the way home,
so plaintively entuned you'd weep to cede
your place in Heaven to him if you had one.

Part II

A Fourteenth-Century Poet's Vision of Christ

A Poetic Drama
for Voices and Instruments
Based on
William Langland's
THE VISION OF WILLIAM
CONCERNING PIERS THE PLOWMAN

To Thomas Beversdorf

PERSONAE

Male Voice— Poet
Soprano— Mary, Peace
Counter Tenor (or Alto)— Imaginative, Holy Spirit, Faith
Tenor— Will, Longinus, Good Samaritan
Baritone— Christ
First Bass— Judas, Satan
Second Bass— Beelzebub
Chorus of Men and Women
Four Female Dancers— Mercy, Peace, Righteousness, Truth
Instruments

Prologue

Introit— Instrumental
>During Introit, Musicians, playing, Chorus, Soloists, and Poet
>march down the aisles and take places on stage.

POET

I have lived long in this land;
>>>my name is Will Langland.
In a cottage in Cornhill,
>>>with my dame and my daughter,
I loll like a Lollard,
>>>a lackadaisical hermit.
Too weak to work
>>>with a scythe or a sickle,
Too long to stoop low,
>>>to labor in fields.

VOICE IN CHORUS

You live then from lands,
>>>or have some wealthy lineage
To find you your food?
>>>For an idle fellow you seem.
Why ought *you* be excused?

POET

When I was yet young,
My father and friends
                sent me to school,
Where from Scripture I learned
                      to search for my soul's sake.
From then have I lingered
                and loafed on in London
With no baggage or bottle
                except my own belly.
The tools that I work with,
                what win me my wages,
Are primer and prayerbook
                and psalter and psalm.
I sing for the sake of
            the givers of almsgifts,
Those that find me my food.
                    Much more than a minstrel
Who lies to make laughter
                rich robes I deserve,
For you tillers and toilers
                I provide with rare Truth.
By the Law of Leviticus
              our dear Lord ordained
That weak poets and prophets,
                  before working and winning,
Should serve Christ by sitting
                and dreaming and singing.
Rebuke me not wrongly,
              for I read in my conscience
What Christ would I work.
                And of him I have hope
Of a gobbet of grace,
              as I link my lewd letters,
That all time from my time
              some profit shall take.

[98]

Part I

Sanctus — Instrumental

POET

In the season of springtime
                 when soft shone the sunshine,
I wandered this wide world
                 with wonders to meet.
And my wits waxed and waned
                 so men held me a madman.
All the folk that I found
                 full often I asked them:

TENOR — WILL

Can any man answer—
                 where is Christ on this earth?

POET

And none could say surely
                 where our Saviour was staying.
Till Friday at forenoon
                 a marvel befell me,
As meatless and moneyless
                 in Malvern's high hills
I lay by a brook bank,
                 refreshing and resting,

Soon falling asleep.
And slumbering fashioned
The most marvelous dream
a man ever dared.
How reason was ravished
in the land of my longing,
In my mirroring mind
now I meditate much.

Fanfare— Instrumental

POET

Of a man I took heed,
like a hermit's his habit,
His shepherd's coat spotted,
with sundry rags patched,
Barefoot and barepated.
He whispered:

COUNTER TENOR— IMAGINATIVE
Will Langland!

Imaginative is my name.
Never am I idle,
Though I sit by myself.
In sickness and health
Have I followed you faithfully
these five and forty winters.
Many a time have I moved you
to muse on your doom.
Years fast disappear,
and few yet to come.

POET

Then I knelt on my knees
and I beat on my breast,

Weeping and wailing
>> I prayed of his pity:

TENOR— WILL

For kindness and courtesy
>> teach me of Christ
That his will I might work,
>> which wrought me a man.
To no treasure direct me,
>> but tell me this truth
To save my sick soul:
>> Where on earth lies Love's Lord?

COUNTER TENOR— IMAGINATIVE

Love, truly to tell,
>> hangs high on a tree.
Mercy, the mother root;
>> the middle stock, Pity.
The leaves are of Loveliness;
>> the blossoms, of Beauty.
Through God and his goodness
>> Love grows— the fruit.

TENOR— WILL

Ten thousands of miles
>> would I travel to taste it;
For my fill of that fruit
>> would forsake other food.
Can you help me to find
>> where this flowering tree flourishes?

COUNTER TENOR— IMAGINATIVE

It grows in a garden
>> that God himself molded
In the midst of man's body—
>> Heart call we that meadow.

And man's will is free
                    to manage this farm.
Christ offers as gardener
                    to glebe it and glean it.

Pastorale— Instrumental

POET

For joy at the sound of
                    the name Jesus I swooned.
And lay long in a stupor
                    till he showed me the spot
Where towered a tree.
                    Fruit studded the top.
For my pleasure I prayed him:

TENOR— WILL

                    Please pluck me some fruit;
I would slake my dry soul
                    and suck its sweet juice.

POET

Then he shook; the tree shivered;
                    fruit fell to the ground.

FIRST BASS

But Satan quick stole it,
                    he snatched that fruit swiftly,
And hid it for hoard
                    deep in darkness and dread.

Ave— Instrumental

CHORUS WOMEN

The Spirit of Holiness
                    suddenly spoke

To a maid called mild Mary;
                    she was meek and untouched.

COUNTER TENOR— HOLY SPIRIT
One Jesus, a King's Son,
                    must sleep in your chamber
Till God's fruit shall flower,
                    shall rise and be ripe.
In time shall this Jesus
                    by judgment in jousting
Prove who the fruit's owner—
                    the Fiend or his Father.

CHORUS WOMEN
This mild-mannered maid
                    the messenger greeted
And said to him meekly:

SOPRANO— MARY
                    Lo, I am his handmaiden.
Without any withholding
                    will I work my Lord's will.

POET
Thus God begat Christ
                    of his own will and goodness,
Became man of a maiden,
                    mankind to save.
Through the grace of the Godhead
                    Mary waxed great with child.
In the womb of this woman
                    Jesus lay forty weeks.

Nativity— Instrumental

CHORUS

This boy then was born.

                Out blazed a bright star,

And the wise of this world

                  with one wit agreed

That a baby was born

                in Bethlehem city

Who man's soul should save

                  and sin should destroy.

BARITONE— CHRIST

He grew to a gallant,

                he gripped knightly weapons

To fight with the Fiend

              when the full time arrived.

SECOND BASS

Then Caiaphas consorted

              with the chiefs of his clique;

To do Christ to death,

              night and day they contrived it.

Part II

When some Jews had a wedding
                     without wine, this youth Jesus
Poured wine out of water,
                the Apostles were witness.
Then leaving his mother
             and living alone,
Made lame men leap lightly,
                brought light to the blind.
And fed with two fishes,
              with barley loaves five,
Men sorely starving,
           six thousand or more.
Dammed ears he undid,
           the dumb he gave tongues.
He healed and he helped
            the hurt and the harmed.
All those that were sick
            he succored and surgeoned—
The perfect practitioner
           if any plague periled.
Both measles and mumps,
             both burning and bleeding,

He slaked them and staunched them;
                                    and considered it small,
Save when he touched Lazarus,
                        who was tucked in a tomb,
For three days lay dead—
                    made him quiver with quickness.
All said at that time
                who saw that weird sight:

CHORUS

He is leech of all life,
                true Lord of the living.

POET

Lo, he succored and surgeoned
                    his own life to save;
Should the enemy hurt him,
                        himself he would heal.
He was called in that country
                        by gentle and common
For the deeds that he did them—

CHORUS
                David's son, Jesus!

POET

For David was doughtiest
                of earls in *his* day.

Fanfare— Instrumental

POET

Then I saw a Samaritan
                sitting on a mule,
Coming from that country
                    men call Jericho

To a joust at Jerusalem.
                          And just then he chanced on
A man who was waylaid,
                          sore wounded by thieves.
No step could he stagger,
                          nor stir hand nor foot,
Nor himself help at all;
                          he seemed half alive.
He was naked as a needle,
                          with none nigh to aid him.
No sooner the Samaritan
                          caught sight of this victim,
He alit from his mule,
                          in his arms him uplifted.
By the pus he perceived
                          his peril of death.
So he hurried to his bottles,
                          hastened back to the hurt one.
With wine and with oil
                          his worst wounds he washed.
In his lap then he laid him,
                          embalmed him and bound him,
Led him forth on his mule
                          some four miles or five,
Quartered him at an inn;
                          of the host he inquired:

TENOR— GOOD SAMARITAN
Will you keep him with courtesy
                          till I come from this joust?
Lo, here is some silver
                          for a salve for his sores.
What more he demands
                          I shall make good hereafter.

CHORUS WOMEN

And rushed to Jerusalem;

in the right way he rode.

CHORUS MEN

The peers plotted against Jesus,

they juggled the law,

Claimed our Saviour worked witchcraft

by the will of the Devil.

BARITONE— CHRIST

Then I charge you are churls

and your children churls too,

And Satan your champion.

Lo, I chose to save you,

So I fed you with fishes

and barley loaves five.

CHORUS

This champion spoke manfully

and made them a challenge;

He whacked them with whips,

he battered the booths

Of the sellers and changers

in church; then he said:

BARITONE— CHRIST

I shall tear down this temple

and trample these stones;

Ere three days have passed,

I shall pile a new pattern.

SECOND BASS

Then Caiaphas consorted

with the chiefs of his clique;

To do Christ to death,

night and day they contrived it.

POET

One resembling the Samaritan
                    sat on a donkey.
Without spurs, without spear,
                    to Jerusalem sped.
A youth full of daring,
                    he yearned to be dubbed,
To win himself spurs
                    and a sword and a shield.
Like a herald of arms
                    when a hero appears,
Faith shouted from a dais:

COUNTER TENOR— FAITH
Hail, Son of David!

Fanfare— Instrumental

POET

The old Jews of Jerusalem
                    sang for great joy:

CHORUS

Hosanna to him,
                    our Messiah is here!

POET

Then I spoke up to Faith:

TENOR— WILL
            All this stir— what's it for?
Who will joust at Jerusalem?

COUNTER TENOR— FAITH
                    Why, Jesus the gentle,
To fetch what the Fiend stole,
                    the fruit of the tree.

[109]

TENOR— WILL

Who will joust against Jesus,
  are they Romans or Jews?

COUNTER TENOR— FAITH

The fierce Fiend himself,
  the false one, the foul.
He shall dent Jesus sorely,
  shall deal him dire blows.
Yet shall death not destroy him.
  When three days are done,
He shall fetch from the Fiend
  all the fruit that he filched.

CHORUS MEN

The peers plotted against Jesus,
  they juggled the law,
Claimed our Saviour worked witchcraft
  by the will of the Devil.

Lavabo— Instrumental

POET

It befell before Friday,
  one day before Passover,
With his fingers and water
  he washed his friends' feet.
Then sitting at supper
  he uttered his sorrow:

Communion— Instrumental

BARITONE— CHRIST

A disciple has sold me,
  a saviour for silver.
His ransom— he'll rue it.

[110]

POET
Then Judas to Jesus:

FIRST BASS— JUDAS
Not so, Lord, have I.

POET
To him spoke our Saviour:

BARITONE— CHRIST
Lo, so have you said it.

POET
To his work went that wicked one
And told by what token
they might know Christ and take him.
Then shouted that rascal:

FIRST BASS— JUDAS
Hail, Rabbi!

POET
right to him,
And kissing him caused him
to be captured and killed.
Then Jesus to Judas,
to that churl spoke the champion:

BARITONE— CHRIST
In your saying so fair
foul falseness I find;
Yes, guile in your greeting
and gall in your gladness.
A mirror to mankind,
you shall gull many more.
But the worst of your wickedness
shall work on yourself.

[111]

CHORUS MEN

Thursday at nightfall
> this knight was nabbed naughtily;
A king taken captive,
> he was bound by the barons,
Through Judas was jeopardized—
> Lord Jesus his name.

BARITONE— CHRIST

Though by trick and by treason
> I am taken unknightly,
My retainers, I pray you,
> in peace let depart.

POET

Then came Pontius Pilate,
> with a mad mess of people,
To judge between Jesus
> and his judges the right.

CHORUS BASSES

The robber Barabbas—
> now pardon, parole him!

CHORUS TENORS

This Nazarene threatened
> to trample our Temple,
One day to destroy it.
> You must doom him to death!

POET

Out cried a cruel captain:

SECOND BASS

Crucify! Him I warrant a witch.

Yelled another fierce knave:

TENOR
Nail him up, nail him up!

POET
And of keen-cutting thorns
               he thatched a thonged crown;
Like a garland then laid it
               on our Lord, and he laughed.
Sharp reeds in the Saviour
               those rascals then rammed;
They tacked him up naked
               with nails on the tree.
A pole dipped in poison
               they pressed to his lips,
Bid him drink his death wine.
               Jesus drank his full doom.

SECOND BASS
If you truly be Christ,
               King's son, as you claim,
And if you be subtle,
               now save your own self,
Come down from that cross.
               Then can we confess
That life loves you dearly,
               will not let you die.

BARITONE— CHRIST
Consummatum est . . .

POET
cried Christ, then he swooned.

[113]

CHORUS WOMEN

Piteously and pale,
        like a poor prisoner dying,
The Lord of life and light
        his eyes together laid.

SOPRANO

This was the cutting of care's knot,
        the oncoming of rest.

Part III

CHORUS MEN

For dread the day withdrew
                            and dark became the sun.
Walls wibbled and wobbled
                            and all the world quaked.
Dead men by the din
                    were drummed up from their graves.

POET

A corpse told why that tempest
                            a long time endured:

BASS FROM CHORUS

For a bitterly fought battle,
                        betide life, betide death,
Rages in this rain swirl—
                        one shall ruin the other.
For sure no man shall know
                        which shall be the master
Before Sunday at sunrise . . .

POET
then sank back in earth.

[115]

CHORUS WOMEN

Some said he was God's son
                            so softly to die.

CHORUS MEN

Some called him a witch.

BASS IN CHORUS
                 Wise we weigh whether

He be full dead or not
                   before we unnail him.

POET

Two thieves then they lofted
                        alongside our Liege Lord.
And a captain came forth
                      and cracked those churls' bones.
But no baron was bold
                  to mangle *his* body,
For Christ was a knight,
                     courageous, a King's son.
There came, though, a squire,
                         with a keen-spitted spear,
Longinus, our lore says,
                      who had long lacked his sight.
Before soldiers and citizens
                          was he led unsuspecting,
Unwitting was handed
                  a weapon to wield,
A lance in his left hand
                      for injuring Jesus.
This boy who was blind
                   pierced our Lord through the loins.

Kyrie— Instrumental

[116]

POET

Blood sprung by that shaft
                    unspeared the lad's eyes.
To his knees fell that squire,
                    sore sighing he spoke:

TENOR— LONGINUS

My will never willed
                    that I wound you, my Master.
This wrong I have wrought—
                    I rue it already.
With pity and pardon
                    now shower me, Saviour.

POET

For the first time rained tears
                    from his radiant eyes.

SOPRANO

Many ladies so lovely,
                    many knights so beloved
Then swooned as if dead,
                    for death's dints they sorrowed.

CHORUS WOMEN

And lo! how the sun
                    locked up all her light
For the sight of him suffering
                    who made sun and stars.

CHORUS

The earth for the heaviness
                    he had to heave under
Quivered like a quick thing,
                    the very rocks quaked.

[117]

CHORUS MEN

No, Hell could not hold
                    for the hurt of him hanging.

POET

So shall Lucifer learn,
                    full loth though he be,
That Jesus the Giant
                    engendered an engine
To batter and beat him
                    that bore off the fruit.

COUNTER TENOR

See, a spirit speaks Hellward,
                    a sound swathed in light:

Fanfare— Instrumental

BARITONE— CHRIST

Proud prince of this place,
                    unpin these speared gates!
Here comes for his kinsmen
                    that King who is Glory.

POET

Then sighing sad Satan
                    spoke to his gang:

FIRST BASS— SATAN

I remember this light;
                    it led from us Lazarus.
Full well now I realize
                    some new woe awaits us.
If this King enters in,
                    mankind he will carry

To which place he pleases;
                    and us will imprison.
Prophets and patriarchs
                    have promised these people
That a Lord of such light
                    should lead them all hence.
By right and by reason
                    these wretches are mine.
God justly doomed them,
                    he himself spoke it,
The highest in Heaven:

COUNTER TENOR— THE LORD GOD
If Adam the fruit eat,
All men must die,
                    must dwell with the Devil.

POET
To Satan, Beelzebub:

SECOND BASS— BEELZEBUB
I am sorry to say it
But you got them by guile,
                    broke into God's garden
In the guise of a serpent,
                    smiling and slithering,
Egged innocent Eve on
                    to eat while alone.
Of treason the text
                    of the tale that you told her.
What is gotten by guile
                    is not rightly gained.
No, God was not gulled,
                    not by treachery tricked.

In my heart now I know
                    that this knight will reclaim them.
For see where a beam
                    comes sailing swift toward us,
With great light and glory—
                    that Lord I believe it.
Far better not be than
                    abide his bright look.
Alas, through your lies, Lucifer,
                    lost is our prey.
First we fell through your falseness
                    from Heaven so high;
Believing your lying,
                    we leaped from that place.
Through your tricks it turns out
                    we lose Adam and Eve,
Must waive all our lordship
                    of water and land.

POET
That light called:

BARITONE— CHRIST
Unlock!

POET
But Lucifer bellowed:

FIRST BASS— SATAN
What knight dares this knocking,
                    what lord of what land?

POET
Then soon spoke the light:

BARITONE— CHRIST
Lord of life am I called,

The King of great glory,

the knight men name Jesus.

Dim dukes of this dungeon,

undo these fast gates

That Christ may come in,

the King's son of Heaven.

CHORUS MEN
With that breath was Hell broken,

burst the bars wrought by Belial.

The gates opened gladly

for prophets and patriarchs.

From the look of that light

was Lucifer blinded.

POET
Who loved their Liege Lord

that light lifted up;

Saying to Satan:

BARITONE— CHRIST
Myself am amend

For the souls that have sinned;

I claim them recaptured.

Begins now your guile

against you to turn,

And my grace to grow

more gallant toward men.

The bitters you brewed

you shall savor yourself.

As doctor of death

now drink your own dose.

But I, Lord of life,

I instigate Love.

[121]

For Love this dark Friday
                    I died on the tree.
Who quaff his sweet juice,
                    Jesus quenches from sin.
A king is unkind
                    not to save his close kin.
Flesh may not suffer
                    flesh to be sick,
Blood not see blood
                    bleed and not staunch it.
Your lying, Lord Lucifer,
                    which you lisped unto Eve—
Abide it now bitterly.

CHORUS MEN
                    Christ bound him with chains.
Belial and Beelzebub
                    and more hid in holes,
On our Lord dared not look,
                    his light was too bold.
But Christ found them and fetched them,
                    punished them as he promised.

COUNTER TENOR
Then hosts in high Heaven
                    harped and sang songs.

Carole— Instrumental

POET
And I saw where a woman
                    walked in from the West;
That maid was named Mercy,
                    in meekness adorned.
And her sister I saw
                    traipsing softly from East,

[122]

A comely bright creature—
                    Truth was she called.
From the nip of the North
                    I saw Righteousness running—
Sweet was her mien.
                    And I saw toward the South
Where Peace approached quickly;
                    of patience her clothes.

Pax— Instrumental

POET
When Peace clothed in patience
                    approached her three sisters,
Righteousness reverenced
                    her robe for its richness,
Then asked her to answer:

CONTRALTO IN CHORUS— RIGHTEOUSNESS
                    To what place are you posting,
Garbed in garments so gay,
                    and whom will you greet there?

SOPRANO— PEACE
I am wending my way
                    to welcome those wanderers
Who by dint of the Devil
                    lay dungeoned in Hell—
Adam and Eve
            and Moses and more.
Christ out of courtesy
            has championed their cause.

SOPRANO IN CHORUS— TRUTH
To be named knight is fair—
                    to him shall men kneel.

CONTRALTO IN CHORUS— RIGHTEOUSNESS
To be called king is fairer—
> he knights can create.

CONTRALTO IN CHORUS— MERCY
To be conqueror called—
> that comes of great gallantry,

Both hardness of hand
> and gentleness of heart.

SOPRANO— PEACE
And now let us dance, sisters,
> dance till this day dawns,

For the judgment has Jesus
> enjoyed in his jousting.

POET
The Heavenly hosts
> then trumpeted triumph.

Sang loud songs to love:

CHORUS
Te Deum laudamus!

Carole— Instrumental and Dance

POET
Till the dawning of Sunday
> these damsels kept dancing,

When a strong-handed angel
> heaved the stone from the tomb.

And a racing retainer
> saw the rock rolled asunder.

Mary Maudlin in the garden
> met Jesus, the Gardener;

In his Godhead he greeted
                    his gallants in Galilee,
He showed himself living,
                    their leader beloved.

CHORUS

Christus resurgens!

Alleluia— Instrumental and Chorus

POET
                Bells rang the Resurrection,
Clanging awoke me.
                    From my eyes wiping water,
In our cottage in Cornhill,
                    the crossroads of London,
I called my wife Kit
                    and Kalotté my daughter:

TENOR— WILL
Arise now and reverence
                    Christ's resurrection;
Come creep on your knees
                    to the Cross, kneel and kiss it.
For Christ's blessed body
                    it bore for our booty;
Thus finished the Fiend.
                    Lo, such is its force
May no grisly ghost
                    glide where it glistens.

POET
I have lived long in this land;
                    my name is Will Langland.

The Passion of Christ
                        once clearly was pictured
In my mirroring mind.
                        High in Malvern I dreamed it.

Benediction— Instrumental

CHORUS

Now must we all love,
                        learn to leave off all other.
We beseech for all sinners
                        our Saviour's glad grace.

Recessional— Instrumental

During Recessional, Poet, Soloists, Chorus, and Musicians, play-
ing, march out the aisles.